Charlie Goes to Paris

A Dog's Adventure

Table of Contents

CHAPTER 11: CONCLUSION 45

© Copyright 2023 - All rights reserved.

Introduction

In a cozy little house nestled at the heart of a bustling town, there lived a most delightful character - Charlie, a playful and spirited Cavalier King Charles Spaniel. With velvety ears that danced as he pranced and eyes that sparkled like stars, Charlie was a true bundle of joy. His beautiful long fur with white and black patches, and his cute little caramel eyebrows, were as soft as a cloud, inviting anyone he met to reach down and give him a gentle pat.

But what made Charlie truly special was his insatiable curiosity and boundless enthusiasm for life. Every day was an opportunity for a new adventure, a chance to explore the world around him. From chasing butterflies in the sunlit garden to embarking on imaginary quests through the living room, Charlie's everyday antics were nothing short of magical.

As the sun rose each morning, Charlie would stretch his paws and wag his tail, eager to see what the world had in store. He was a loyal companion, a furry friend who had stolen the hearts of all who knew him. From the postman to the children who played in the park, Charlie was adored by everyone in the neighborhood.

And so, our story begins not in the far-off city of Paris, but right here, in the midst of Charlie's charming hometown. Join us as we peel back the curtain on Charlie's extraordinary life and the grand adventure that would soon take him on a journey beyond his wildest dreams. Through the pages of this book, you'll discover the magic that comes alive when a curious dog sets his sights on the enchanting city of Paris.

So, dear reader, get ready to embark on a heartwarming tale of friendship, discovery, and the joy of chasing dreams. As we turn the page, we invite you to step into Charlie's world and experience the wonder that awaits you. After all, every grand adventure begins with a single paw step, and Charlie invites you to come along on his trip of a lifetime.

Chapter 1:

Meet Charlie: A Playful Cavalier King Charles Spaniel

In a charming little house with a white picket fence, nestled amidst a neighborhood that buzzed with life, there lived an enchanting creature named Charlie. Charlie was no ordinary dog; he was a Cavalier King Charles Spaniel, a breed known for its elegance, loyalty and loving, cheerful disposition.

With fur as soft as silk and eyes that twinkled with mischief, Charlie was a sight to behold. His coat was a beautiful blend of rich onyx black and pristine white, perfectly complementing the caramel eyebrows and wafts of long fur with gentle waves that cascaded down his back. His long, feathery ears were a source of endless entertainment, bouncing like fluffy pendulums with every step he took.

But it was Charlie's personality that truly stole the show. He embodied the spirit of what the French call "joie de vivre" (The joy of living). His days were spent frolicking in the sun-drenched yard, chasing after his own shadow, and playing an endless game of fetch with his beloved tennis ball. He had an uncanny ability to turn even the most mundane objects into thrilling toys: a fallen leaf became a treasure to chase, and a discarded cardboard box transformed into a magical castle.

Charlie's charm extended beyond his energetic antics. He had an uncanny sense of when someone needed a furry friend to cuddle with. If a gloomy day cast a shadow over the town, Charlie would trot over to offer a sympathetic gaze and a warm, comforting nuzzle. His presence alone had the power to bring smiles to faces and mend broken hearts.

As you flip through the pages of this book, you'll have the pleasure of getting to know Charlie up close and personal. You'll witness his heartwarming interactions with the people of the town, his unbreakable bond with his family, and the joy he brought to everyone he met. But our tale doesn't stop here—no, this is just the beginning of an extraordinary journey that will take Charlie far beyond the white picket fence, to a place where dreams come true.

Setting the Stage: Charlie's Everyday Adventures

Amidst the backdrop of the picturesque town, Charlie's everyday adventures painted a vibrant portrait of a life filled with joy and wonder. From sunrise to sunset, Charlie's days were a whirlwind of excitement, exploration, and connection.

Each morning, as the sun peeked over the horizon, Charlie's eyes would flutter open, and his tail would start to wag as if powered by pure enthusiasm. It was as though he couldn't wait to dive headfirst into the new day, ready to uncover whatever surprises it held.

Charlie's routine was a masterpiece of joyful chaos. Breakfast was a delightful dance around his food bowl, his tail swaying in rhythm with every eager bite. Then, with energy levels fully charged, he'd embark on a series of playful escapades that could turn even the most ordinary backyard into a realm of endless possibilities.

The garden became his kingdom, a realm to be explored and conquered. Charlie would dart through bushes, paws thudding against the earth as he chased imaginary foes and falling leaves. He'd leap through sprinklers, his laughter-like barks harmonizing with the tinkling water. And when the birds joined in with their melodies, Charlie's own joyful yips created an impromptu symphony.

But Charlie's adventures were not confined to the yard alone. He was a social butterfly, flitting from one encounter to another, leaving a trail of smiles wherever he went. A brief encounter with the mail carrier turned into a friendly game of tag, and a walk to the park became a whirlwind of tail-wagging greetings with other four-legged friends.

Through these everyday escapades, Charlie's infectious spirit and boundless enthusiasm painted a vivid tapestry of life's simple pleasures. His antics reminded everyone that even in the midst of busy schedules and grown-up worries, there was always time to pause, play, and embrace the magic of the present moment.

As you journey through the pages ahead, you'll experience firsthand the whimsy and delight that defined Charlie's days. But hold onto your seat, for Charlie's tale is about to take a most unexpected turn—a turn that will lead him on a grand adventure to a city known for its charm and elegance: Paris.

Chapter 2:

A Dream Unveiled

Charlie's heart was a treasure chest of dreams, each one brimming with possibilities and adventures waiting to be explored. One lazy afternoon, as golden sunlight streamed through the windows and danced across the floor, Charlie stumbled upon a magical key that would unlock one of these cherished dreams.

Nestled among a pile of books, one particular tome caught Charlie's attention. Its cover was adorned with a stunning painting of an iconic tower that seemed to reach for the sky. The title read "Paris: City of Wonders." With curiosity piqued, Charlie gingerly pawed at the pages, as if he could almost feel the magic seeping through the paper.

Charlie's Curiosity: Discovering Paris Through a Book

As Charlie delved into the pages of the book, he was whisked away on a literary adventure that transported him to the heart of Paris. He walked along the cobbled streets, his paws clicking against the stones, and marveled at the elegant architecture that surrounded him. The vivid descriptions painted images in his mind—bustling cafes with the aroma of freshly baked croissants, the sparkling waters of the Seine River, and the breathtaking beauty of the Eiffel Tower.

With each page turned, Charlie's curiosity grew. He devoured stories of artists and poets who had found inspiration on these very streets, and he imagined himself joining their ranks, his tail wagging in rhythm to the beat of the city. The more he read, the more his desire to experience Paris firsthand ignited, like a spark growing into a blazing fire.

Dreaming Big: Charlie's Desire to Visit Paris

Night after night, Charlie's dreams were filled with visions of Paris. He would wander through the city's enchanting neighborhoods, his paws leaving pawprints on the boulevards. He'd gaze up at the twinkling lights of the Eiffel Tower, feeling as though he could almost touch the stars. And in these dreams, Charlie wasn't just a dog—he was a

gallant explorer, a true adventurer, ready to embrace all the wonders that Paris had to offer.

But as the sun rose each morning, Charlie would awaken, his heart a mix of excitement and longing. He would sit by the window, his eyes fixed on the horizon, and imagine the day when he could trade his dreams for reality. He knew that Paris wasn't just a distant city—it was a dream waiting to be fulfilled, a story waiting to be written, and Charlie was determined to be the one to write it.

With every turn of the page, Charlie's dream grew stronger, his determination more resolute. Join us as we follow Charlie on a journey that will take him from the pages of a book to the very heart of the City of Light. For dreams, when fueled by passion and unwavering hope, have a way of transforming into the most extraordinary adventures. Charlie believed the old saying "Where there is a will, there is a way" and he was determined to find a way to Paris.

Chapter 3:

Paws on the Ground

The anticipation in the air was palpable as Charlie's dream of visiting Paris edged closer to reality. One day, as he was browsing through his Paris book, he came upon a contest for a free trip to Paris. One lucky contestant would be selected to participate in a cooking class and then provide their review of the class. His little paws seemed to dance with excitement, his tail a constant blur of wagging. The once-distant city had now become a beacon of hope. He quickly, without a second thought, entered the contest hoping he would be chosen to take the class and give his review. In a few days, he was contacted and miraculously, Charlie was chosen as the winner, hooray, he was going to Paris. His dream had come true!

Charlie's Journey Begins: Packing and Preparations

With a determined glint in his eyes, Charlie's preparations for the journey commenced. The living room turned into a whirlwind of activity as he trotted back and forth, gathering his most cherished belongings. His favorite tennis ball was a must, as were his coziest blanket and a picture of his family, a reminder of the love he carried with him.

Charlie's suitcase, a miniature marvel in itself, was filled to the brim. Tucked away were treats, a small bowl for water, and a toy that squeaked with a sound that reminded him of home. As he zipped up

the bag, Charlie took one last look around his room, his heart full of excitement and a touch of nostalgia.

The night before his departure, Charlie curled up in his bed, his dreams a tapestry of Parisian adventures. He imagined himself strolling down the Seine, the scent of fresh baguettes wafting through the air. He envisioned chasing pigeons near the Eiffel Tower and sipping from a dainty bowl of water at a charming café, and as the moonlit night wrapped him in a gentle embrace, Charlie's soft snores carried the promise of the journey ahead.

Boarding the Plane: Charlie's First Flight Adventure

Morning arrived with a chorus of birdsong, and with it, the realization that the moment Charlie had been waiting for was finally here. The bustling airport, a symphony of voices and rolling suitcases, seemed like a whirlwind of activity that only heightened Charlie's excitement.

Charlie's heart raced as he stood in line, his tail swishing back and forth like a metronome keeping time with his pulse. The sound of the boarding announcement sent a thrill through his furry frame. It was time to take his first steps toward Paris.

The airplane cabin was a new world, a mix of curious scents and gentle hums. Charlie's ears perked up as he settled into his designated spot by the window. His eyes widened as the plane's engines roared to life, and

he felt a gentle rumble beneath his paws as the aircraft taxied down the
runway.

As the plane lifted off the ground, Charlie's heart soared. He pressed his nose against the window, his breath fogging the glass as he watched his hometown shrink into a patchwork of green and brown. The world outside transformed into a canvas of clouds, and Charlie's imagination painted the skies with images of croissants, berets, and the iconic Eiffel Tower.

The hours passed like a dream as Charlie dozed in his cozy spot, his
dreams a medley of Parisian adventures and new friendships waiting to
be forged. And as the plane descended toward its destination, Charlie's
heart raced with anticipation, for he knew that just beyond the horizon
lay the magical city he had dreamed of for so long.

Chapter 4

Bonjour, Paris!

The moment the airplane's wheels touched the runway, Charlie's heart danced with joy. He was in Paris, the city that had lived within his dreams and now unfolded before his very eyes. As he stepped out of the plane, his paws met the ground of a place that felt both familiar and enchantingly new.

Touchdown in France: Charlie Arrives in Paris

A gentle breeze carried the scent of freshly baked bread and blooming flowers, embracing Charlie in a warm welcome. The architecture that surrounded him was a masterpiece of intricate details and elegant designs. His eyes widened at the sight of the sprawling cityscape, a symphony of colors and shapes that stretched to the horizon.

Charlie walked through the airport, and stepped outside, the magic of Paris embracing him. The iconic Eiffel Tower stood tall against the sky, a sight that made Charlie's heart skip a beat. Its iron lattice seemed to whisper tales of grandeur and history, and Charlie couldn't help but gaze in awe.

New Scents and Sights: Charlie's Exploration of the City

With each step, Charlie's senses were treated to a sensory feast. The aroma of buttery croissants wafted from nearby cafes, and the rhythmic chatter of French filled the air. He could not resist, he had to stop for a caffe latte and a mouthwatering croissant. He closed his eyes and breathed in the City of Paris, the place he had longed for, he was finally here.

After his brief break, Charlie's ears perked up and he trotted down the charming streets lined with boutiques and flower shops. His eyes darted left and right, eager to take in every detail.

In a quiet park, Charlie discovered the Seine River, its waters reflecting the elegance of the city. He watched as boats glided by, their wakes sending ripples of excitement through his furry frame. He jumped on board a little blue boat for a quick ride, almost tipping it over. He gazed into the river, saw his own reflection and smiled. After his boat ride he continued his journey to discover Paris. Charlie's paws itched to explore every nook and cranny, to leave his mark on the pathways that countless others had walked.

At a bustling square, Charlie found himself amidst street performers and artists, their talents on display for all to see. He tilted his head at a mime, mimicking its antics with a playful twirl. The sights and sounds of Paris became a symphony of experiences, and Charlie's heart swelled with gratitude for the journey that had brought him here.

As the sun began to dip below the horizon, casting a warm golden glow over the city, Charlie realized that he was no longer just dreaming. Paris was now his reality, a canvas upon which he could paint his own adventures. With every passing moment, he embraced the beauty of the city and the endless possibilities that lay ahead.

Culinary Adventures in Paris

On his second evening in Paris he was to take the cooking class. Charlie's heart raced with a mixture of excitement and nervous anticipation as he stood outside a charming cooking school in the heart of Paris. The grand prize of his journey had been winning a trip to this magical city, and part of the experience included taking this cooking class and leaving his review. Charlie's tail wagged energetically, his paws

eager to step into a world of flavors and aromas unlike anything he had experienced before. The cooking school was a cozy haven, its interior adorned with colorful aprons, gleaming utensils, and the promise of culinary delights. Charlie's instructor, a warm and friendly chef named Madame Lucie, welcomed him with a cheerful smile and a playful pat on the head. The other participants in the class—humans and a few fellow canine travelers—greeted Charlie with wagging tails and friendly sniffs.

The day's menu was a medley of French classics—coq au vin, ratatouille, and a decadent chocolate mousse for dessert. Charlie's heart raced as he watched Madame Lucie demonstrate each step with precision and passion. His nose twitched as the aromas of fresh herbs, sizzling onions, and simmering sauces filled the air, creating a symphony of scents that awakened his senses.

With his apron securely fastened and his chef's hat perched atop his head, Charlie eagerly joined the cooking process. He chopped vegetables with concentration, his tongue peeking out in adorable determination. He helped stir pots with his little paws, his tail wagging as he contributed to the creation of each dish. The

camaraderie among the participants and the joy of working side by side made the experience all the more delightful.

As the final touches were added to each dish, Charlie's mouth watered in anticipation. The coq au vin was a masterpiece of tender chicken and rich red wine sauce, the ratatouille a colorful mosaic of flavors, and the chocolate mousse a velvety indulgence that melted on the tongue. With each bite, Charlie tasted the essence of Paris, a city that embraced him not just with its sights and sounds, but also with its culinary artistry.

The Review: Charlie's Culinary Adventure

As Charlie savored the last spoonful of chocolate mousse, he couldn't help but reflect on the cooking class that had become an unforgettable part of his Parisian journey. The experience had been a symphony of flavors, a dance of ingredients, and a celebration of culture and community. Madame Lucie's guidance had transformed a group of eager participants into a team of aspiring chefs, each one contributing their own unique touch to the feast.

The class had not only taught Charlie about the art of French cuisine but had also illuminated the joy of collaboration, the beauty of creativity, and the power of sharing a meal with loved ones. Through the laughter, the shared experiences, and the delicious results, Charlie had come to understand that food was more than sustenance—it was a form of expression, a way to connect with others, and a reminder that even in a city as grand as Paris, the most memorable moments were often found in the simplest of pleasures.

And so, with a satisfied belly and a heart full of gratitude, Charlie's review of the cooking class could be summed up in one word— **magnifique**! The experience had added a layer of depth to his Parisian adventure, a layer that was rich with the flavors of friendship, discovery, and the boundless joy of following his dreams.

Chapter 5:

Eiffel Tower Tails

The day after his class he wanted to explore Paris and ended up right in front of The Eiffel Tower. That iconic symbol of Paris stood before Charlie like a majestic giant reaching for the heavens. Its intricate lattice of iron seemed to capture the very essence of the city—graceful, strong, and filled with wonder. As Charlie gazed up at the towering structure, a mixture of awe and excitement swelled within him.

Charlie's Iconic Encounter: Discovering the Eiffel Tower

With each step closer to the Eiffel Tower, Charlie's heart beat faster, a rhythm that matched the cadence of his excitement. The soft rustling

of leaves, the distant laughter of children playing, and the hum of city life seemed to fade into the background, all eclipsed by the towering presence before him. It was as if the world had hushed in reverence, allowing Charlie to forge a personal connection with this iconic monument.

Standing at the base of the Eiffel Tower, Charlie craned his neck and tilted his head back, his gaze traveling up the intricate lattice of iron that stretched toward the heavens. His eyes roamed over every curve and detail, taking in the graceful arches and the delicate tracery that seemed to defy gravity. It was a marvel of human ingenuity, an embodiment of artistry and engineering that left Charlie utterly captivated.

As the elevators ascended and descended the tower's legs, Charlie's eyes followed their graceful movement. They were like jewels in a delicate necklace, each one a testament to the tower's function as both a masterpiece of design and a practical mode of transport. The sight of these elevators seemed to add a touch of life to the tower, a rhythmic pulse that resonated with Charlie's own excitement.

With a flutter of excitement in his chest, Charlie embarked on a journey that would take him to new heights—literally. As he ascended the Eiffel Tower, his paws carried him up the winding path, each step a promise of the breathtaking view that awaited him.

The city of Paris unfolded beneath him like a tapestry, apatchwork of rooftops and streets that seemed to stretch to infinity. The wind tousled his ears and ruffled his fur as he gazed out in wonder, his eyes capturing the essence of a city that sparkled with life. Charlie's heart swelled with a mix of exhilaration and gratitude. This was a moment he would forever treasure his dream had become a reality.

He descends the elevator and gazes back at the iconic structure where the play of sunlight upon the iron lattice adds another layer of magic to this dreamy scene. As he finally tears his gaze away from the tower and continues his journey through Paris, Charlie carries with him the memory of that iconic encounter and realizes even a little Cavalier King Charles Spaniel could stand on the threshold of something extraordinary and achieve a dream.

Making Friends: Charlie's Playdate with Parisian Pooches

As Charlie continued his exploration of Paris, he quickly discovered that the city was not just a place of landmarks and monuments, but also a vibrant community of both humans and furry companions. In a charming park, Charlie's nose twitched with anticipation as he caught the scent of fellow canines.

Curious eyes met Charlie's, and friendly tails wagged in greeting. Charlie's heart soared as he bounded toward a group of Parisian pooches, his tail a blur of excitement. Language barriers melted away as the universal language of play united them all. They chased each other through the grass, exchanged playful barks, and shared stories of their own adventures.

Charlie's joy knew no bounds as he made new friends, each one with their own unique personality and tale to tell. A pretty little Poodle showed him the most beautiful and enchanting carousel, a French Bulldog revealed the best spots for chasing squirrels and a friendly Pomeranian shared a secret garden tucked away from the bustling streets. Amidst shared laughter and shared treats, Charlie felt a sense of belonging that transcended borders.

And so, under the watchful gaze of the Arc de Triomphe, Charlie experienced not only the grandeur of Paris but also the warmth of its community. The Arc, standing tall and proud, seemed to smile approvingly as Charlie's tail wagged in harmony with the rhythm of the city. With every new friend he made, Paris became more than just a destination—it became a home away from home, a place where even a curious canine could find companionship and create cherished memories.

Chapter 6:

Croissant Capers

The aroma of freshly baked croissants wafted through the air like a siren's call, capturing Charlie's senses and leading him on a delectable adventure through the heart of Paris.

Breakfast Adventures: Charlie's Love for Croissants

From the first moment Charlie sank his teeth into a flaky, buttery croissant, his taste buds danced with delight. It was as if each bite carried a piece of the city's essence—a medley of warmth, comfort, and pure indulgence. Whether it was a quaint bakery tucked away on a cobblestone street or a bustling café with outdoor seating, Charlie was on a  mission to sample every croissant the city had to offer.

Morning after morning, Charlie's breakfast escapades became a joyful ritual. He'd trot through charming alleyways, his nose leading the way to a new culinary treasure. With a croissant held gently between his teeth, he'd find a cozy spot to savor each delectable bite, his tail swaying in rhythm with his appreciation for the artistry of French baking.

Chasing Crumbs: Charlie's Escapades in a Parisian Café

One sunny day, Charlie's love for croissants led him to a lively Parisian café. The enticing aroma drew him closer, and with a confident wag of his tail, he strolled in as though he owned the place. The café was a symphony of clinking cups and lively chatter, a backdrop of human and canine companionship that filled Charlie with a sense of belonging. Seated at a table with a view of the bustling street, Charlie observed the flurry of activity around him. As he sipped an espresso and samples pastries, Charlie's keen eyes caught every crumb that fell to the floor. Unable to resist the call of a tasty morsel, he sprang into action, his

paws a blur as he playfully chased the crumbs that dared to escape.

In the heart of that Parisian café, Charlie created memories that were as sweet as the confections he adored. With each crumb chased and every tail wag exchanged, he discovered that his love for croissants was more than a culinary preference—it was a way to connect with the heart of Paris and the people who made the city come alive.

And so, as the sun set over the city of lights, Charlie left the café with his heart full and his belly content, ready to embrace whatever new adventures awaited him on the charming streets of Paris.

Chapter 7:

Seine River Serenade

The next day, Charlie decided to take a stroll along the Seine River, a watery ribbon that weaved through the heart of Paris. The Seine was beckoning to Charlie like a mysterious enchantress, promising tales of romance and adventure. As he walked along the Seine, he discovered a boating tour for visitors to cruise along the river.

He decided it would be a great way to see the city, so he boarded one of the little red boats and secured his position on the deck to begin his tour.

Boating Bonanza: Charlie's Cruise on the Seine River

With a sense of anticipation that matched the gentle lapping of the water against the boat's hull, Charlie embarked on a boating adventure along the Seine. The boat was a vessel of dreams, carrying Charlie on a journey through time and history. While the boat glided along, Charlie's ears perked up, as the gentle breeze and the soft murmurs of the tour guide left a relaxing calm over him as he listened intently to each anecdote and legend adding to the tapestry of the city's past.

Seated on the deck, Charlie felt the cool breeze ruffle his fur and the warmth of the sun kiss his nose. He watched as the city's landmarks passed by—majestic bridges, charming cafes nestled along the riverbanks, and the iconic Notre Dame Cathedral. The Seine seemed to cradle the city in its embrace, and Charlie's heart swelled with a sense of wonder at the beauty that surrounded him. He dozed off and took a short nap before the tour ended and he continued his adventure.

Musical Moments: Charlie's Encounter with a Street Musician

As evening approached, Charlie strolled along the bustling streets of Paris, the city's vibrant energy enveloped him like a joyful melody. It was a symphony of sounds—the laughter of children, the melodious conversations of passersby, and the intoxicating rhythm of life itself.

But amidst this cacophony, another set of notes caught Charlie's attention—the sweet strains of a violin.

Charlie closed his eyes for a moment and took in the music of the city. Like a warm embrace, it guided him toward the young musician. The Violinist played with joy, vigor, passion and romance that resonated in every note, the melody intertwining with the heartbeat of Paris.

As the music swelled, Charlie's surroundings blurred into a whirl of colors and movement as he danced along beside the violinist for a little while. He was no longer just a dog on a Parisian street; he was a dancer, a muse, a participant in a grand performance that united strangers from all walks of life. And as the final notes hung in the air like a promise of shared joy, Charlie knew that these musical moments were more than just entertainment—they were a reminder that in the heart of Paris, magic could be found in the most unexpected places.

Chapter 8:

Louvre Quest

As the sun rose over Paris the next morning, Charlie decided to visit The Louvre, a palace of art and history. The Glass pyramid structure and the museum stood before Charlie like a gateway to a realm of creativity and imagination unlike any other. Its grandeur and elegance seemed to whisper tales of bygone eras, beckoning Charlie to embark on a quest of discovery and wonder.

Artistic Antics: Charlie's Visit to the Louvre Museum

With an air of excitement that matched the fluttering of his ears, Charlie stepped into the hallowed halls of the Louvre. The museum was a treasure trove of masterpieces, each one a testament to the ingenuity and creativity of humanity. As Charlie wandered through the corridors, his eyes danced from one masterpiece to the next, his

tail swaying in tune with the vibrant energy that radiated from each canvas.

In the presence of these works of art, Charlie felt a sense of connection that transcended time and space. He marveled at the brushstrokes that brought scenes to life, the colors that seemed to dance with emotion, and the stories that unfolded with each stroke of the artist's hand. It was as if the paintings were windows into different worlds, and Charlie was a curious explorer gazing through each one.

Puppy Picasso: Charlie's Artistic Interpretation

Amidst the grandeur of the Louvre, Charlie found himself drawn to a blank canvas, a pristine space awaiting his own artistic touch. With a confident wag of his tail, Charlie approached the canvas, his eyes shining with determination. He dipped his paw into a palette of vibrant colors and then onto the canvas, leaving behind a trail of whimsical strokes and playful smudges.

As Charlie's creation took shape, he felt an exhilarating rush of creativity. His paw moved with a sense of purpose, guided by an innate understanding of expression and beauty. The colors blended and swirled, forming a tapestry of shapes and forms that seemed to capture the essence of his Parisian adventure.

When Charlie finally stepped back to admire his masterpiece, he couldn't help but wag his tail in approval. The painting was a reflection of his journey—the Eiffel Tower rising against a pastel sky, the Seine River winding through a cityscape, and a joyful pup, tail wagging, basking in the beauty of it all. In that moment, Charlie realized that art was not just about what one saw, but about the emotions and experiences that flowed through the artist's heart.

And so, as Charlie left the Louvre, his own artistic contribution gracing its walls, he carried with him a newfound appreciation for the world of art and the infinite ways in which it could be interpreted and celebrated. In his own pawprints and strokes, Charlie had become a part of the grand tapestry of creativity that the Louvre embodied—a legacy of artistic expression that would linger in the hearts of all who beheld it.

Montmartre Magic

Montmartre, a charming hilltop neighborhood known as the artist's haven, beckoned to Charlie like a canvas awaiting the touch of a painter's brush. Its cobblestone streets and bohemian spirit promised a unique adventure that would awaken Charlie's senses and ignite his creativity.

Exploring the Artist's Quarter: Charlie's Montmartre Adventure

As Charlie stepped into the lively streets of Montmartre, he was enveloped by a sense of artistic enchantment. The air was thick with the scent of oil paints, and the rhythmic clatter of brushstrokes against canvas created a symphony of creation. Everywhere he looked, Charlie was greeted by colorful stalls and open-air studios, each one a portal to a world of imagination.

Charlie's paws led him up winding staircases and down narrow alleys, his curiosity guiding him toward hidden gems and unexpected encounters. He watched as artists brought scenes to life with vibrant hues, capturing the essence of Paris on their canvases. Charlie felt a kinship with these creators, his own adventures and experiences woven into the fabric of the neighborhood's artistic tapestry.

Pawsitive Memories: Charlie's Souvenir Shopping Spree

In Montmartre's bustling marketplace, Charlie's eyes widened at the sight of a myriad of trinkets and treasures. His tail wagged in rhythm with his excitement as he perused stalls filled with whimsical postcards, dainty trinkets, and vibrant paintings that captured the spirit of the city. Each item seemed to carry a piece of Montmartre's magic, a souvenir of a place where creativity flourished.

Charlie's nose led him to a charming shop filled with handmade treasures. There, he discovered a collection of delicate ceramic figurines, each one a work of art in its own right. Charlie carefully selected a piece that spoke to him—a miniature Eiffel Tower, adorned with intricate details that seemed to mirror the city's elegance.

With his treasure in tow, Charlie continued his exploration, his heart and paws filled with the joy of discovery. As he left Montmartre behind, the memories of his adventure clung to him like paint on a canvas, a reminder that even a playful pup could leave a pawprint on the world of art and creativity.

And so, with a sense of fulfillment and a newfound appreciation for the power of artistic expression, Charlie carried Montmartre's magic with him as he ventured back into the heart of Paris, ready to continue his journey through a city that held boundless opportunities for discovery and wonder.

Chapter 10:

Homeward Bound

The time had come for Charlie to bid adieu to the enchanting city that had captured his heart. As he stood amidst the bustling energy of Paris, his gaze lingered on the familiar landmarks and charming streets that had become his playground. The Seine River sparkled like a ribbon of silver, the Eiffel Tower stood tall and proud, and the cobblestone pathways seemed to whisper tales of his adventures.

Saying Au Revoir: Charlie's Farewell to Paris

With a mixture of gratitude and a touch of melancholy, Charlie took one last stroll through the streets of Paris. Each step felt like a silent conversation with the city, a way of expressing his appreciation for the experiences he had savored and the friendships he had forged.

At a quiet park by the Seine, Charlie sat by the water's edge, his gaze fixed on the horizon.

As the sun dipped below the skyline, casting a warm golden glow over the city, Charlie whispered his farewell to Paris. He promised to carry the memories of his adventures with him, like a treasure tucked away in the depths of his heart. The city had become a part of him, its spirit intertwined with his own, and as he turned to walk away, Charlie knew that his journey was far from over. The lessons he had learned, the friendships he had made, and the love he had felt would continue to guide him, no matter where his paws would lead.

Paris in Charlie's Heart: Cherished Memories

Back in the comfort of his home, Charlie curled up in his favorite spot, his mind a tapestry woven with the threads of Parisian memories. He closed his eyes and felt the breeze of the Seine against his fur, tasted the buttery indulgence of croissants on his tongue, and heard the melodies of street musicians in his ears.

As Charlie's dreams carried him back to the streets of Paris, he realized that the city was not just a place he had visited—it was apart of his story, a chapter etched into his journey. Paris had taught him the beauty of curiosity, the power of friendship, and the magic of following his heart's desires. And so, as Charlie drifted into slumber with a contented sigh, he knew that Paris would forever live on within him, a source of inspiration and a reminder that every adventure, no matter how fleeting, leaves an indelible mark on the soul.

Chapter 11:

Conclusion

Charlie's Return: Sharing Stories with Friends and Family

As Charlie's paws carried him back to the familiar surroundings of home, he couldn't help but feel a sense of bittersweet nostalgia. Paris, with its enchanting streets and heartwarming experiences, had become a cherished part of him. With every wag of his tail and every excited bark, Charlie regaled his friends and family with tales of his Parisian escapades. He painted vivid pictures with his words, bringing to life the magic of the Eiffel Tower, the serenity of the Seine River, and the vibrant energy of the city's streets. His loved ones listened with rapt attention, sharing in his excitement and laughter as he recounted his journey in vivid detail. Charlie's stories became a bridge between his world and theirs, connecting them through shared experiences and igniting a spark of wanderlust in their hearts.

The Endearing Tale of Charlie's Parisian Adventure

And so, dear reader, we reach the end of Charlie's endearing tale—a story of a curious Cavalier King Charles Spaniel who dared to dream and embarked on a journey that would forever shape his spirit. From the playful streets of his hometown to the charming alleyways of Montmartre, from the iconic Eiffel Tower to the tranquil banks of the Seine River, Charlie's adventure was a tapestry woven with threads of curiosity, friendship, and love. He imagined himself as a painting hanging in the Louvre, in that city that he had come to love. Paris was in his heart now and he could not wait to visit again someday.

The Dream Continues:

As Charlie rests his head on his favorite cushion, his heart is brimming with gratitude. He has discovered that the world is a canvas waiting to be explored, and every moment is a stroke of color, every experience a brushstroke that adds depth to the masterpiece of life. Paris may be a place on a map, but to Charlie, it is a state of mind—a reminder that every day is an opportunity for a new adventure, every corner a chance to uncover hidden treasures, and every dream a possibility waiting to unfold.

And so, as we bid adieu to Charlie and his Parisian tale, let us remember that the spirit of adventure lives within us all, just waiting for the moment when we too can follow our hearts, chase our dreams, and create our own stories of wonder and enchantment. After all, the world is vast, and every step is a chance to dance in the rhythm of life's most beautiful melodies.

We leave you with Charlie, curled up in his comfy bed at home once again. As he starts to drift off to sleep, he remembers his time in Paris and how he has become an artist, a chef and a dancer. As he begins to snore softly, he dreams of his next escapade. Where will Charlie's next big adventure take him? Let the dreams begin.